WALKING TO SNAILBEACH

Other Publications by the author

Poetry collections:
Scorpion Days, Rivelin Press, 1982, and Medal Poets Australia, 1987; *Red Marl and Brick*, Littlewood Press, 1985; *Rights of Way*, Unibird Press, 1990; *Travelling Solo*, K.T.Publications, 1995; *No Cure in Tears*, Aireings Publications in conjunction with Carers National,1997; *Owlstone*, Thalia Press, 2002

Novels:
Waters of Time, Century Hutchinson 1988; large print edition, Ulverscroft 1991; *The Keepers*, Virago (Little, Brown), June 1996 and August 1997

Editorial work and Criticism:
Brian Merrikin Hill: Poet and Mentor, Fighting Cock Press, 1999; *The Fairy Band*, by Walter Hill, KT Publications, 1997; *Streets Ahead: The Castleford Renewal Experience,* Yorkshire Art Circus, 1994 (with Brian Lewis); *A Survivor Myself: Experiences of Child Abuse,* Yorkshire Art Circus 1994; *Bewdley Days 1938-54*, Bewdley Civic Society, 1992; *Bramley Band*, Bramley History Society, 1992; *Bramley: the Village that Disappeared*, Bramley History Society, 1983 and subsequent reprints; *Reflections*, Leeds City Council, 1981; *Bramley Short Stories*, Printed Resources Unit for Continuing Education, Leeds, 1980; *The Good Old, Bad Old Days*, Printed Resources Unit for Continuing Education, Leeds, 1980

Senior Editor for the Fighting Cock Press

*With best wishes
from Pauline*

Walking to Snailbeach

SELECTED AND NEW POEMS

≈

PAULINE KIRK

Pauline Kirk

RED BECK PRESS

2004

Walking to Snailbeach is published by
Redbeck Press, 24 Airville Road,
Frizinghall, Bradford, BD9 4HH

Design and print by Tony Ward,
Arc & Throstle Press, Nanholme Mill,
Todmorden, Lancs. OL14 6DA

Copyright © Pauline Kirk 2004

ISBN 1 904338 15 1

Redbeck Press acknowledges financial assistance from the Arts Council England, Yorkshire

Cover design by Wendy Cantell

Some of these poems first appeared in the following journals and anthologies: *Acumen, Aesthetica, Aireings, An Enduring Flame, Arts Yorkshire, A Taste of the Pennine Poets, Cleopatra* (Italy), *Dreamcatcher, Dress of Nettles, East and West Literary Quarterly* (USA), *Endless Mountains Review* (USA), *Essex Countryside, Farmer's Weekly, Fat Chance, Forward Press Top 100 Poets 2002, Gabriel, Hybrid, Incept, Island, La Carta de Oliver* (South America), *Loose Change, Mad Poets Review* (USA), *Mir* (USA), *Mobius Poetry* (USA), *New Hope International, New Hope International Writing, NASA* (USA), *Nikkei* (USA), *Pennine Platform, Pennine Poets Anthology 1966-86, Pennine Tracks, Pennine Twenty Five, The Poetry Church, The Poetry Church Collections 2002 and 2003, Poetry in the Parks, Poems from Portsmouth, Poetry Monash* (Australia), *Poetry Monthly, Poetry Salzburg Review* (Austria), *Psychopoetica, Purple and Green:Poems by 33 Women Poets, Q* (USA), *Second Light Newsletter, Sheaf, Take One Day, Thalia, The World at Our Feet, The Third Half, The New Writer, Ultra Koncise* (USA),*Webbed Skylights of Tall Oaks, Yesterday's Yorkshire.* Also *Radio Leeds, Rumol'do* (CD), *Pickings: Samples of Poetry from NHI Publications* (website). 'The Horsforth Ballad' was performed in *On Borrowed Time* by the Triple Time Theatre Company, 1993 and 1994.

I am grateful for a Bursary and a 'New Beginnings Award', from Yorkshire Arts (1980 and 1994).

CONTENTS

Foreword **by Mary Sheepshanks**

SELECTED POEMS
Scorpion Days and Red Marl and Brick
Scorpion Days / 13
Walking to Snailbeach / 14
Inheritance / 15
Slow Spring / 16
On Southlake Crescent / 16
Almost a Love Song / 17
Parkinsons' Disease / 18
From Plague Village / 19
Cripple Syke / 20
Epiphany / 21
Miner's Song: the Horsforth Ballad / 22
Nativity Play / 24
Turtles / 25
Muttonbirds / 26

Rights of Way and Travelling Solo
Celebration / 29
December / 30
Brontë Bridge / 31
Miss Templeton / 32
Nailhouse / 33
Faith Tea / 34
Marsden Memorial / 35
Requiem for an Enemy / 36
Outbreak of War / 37
Refugees / 38
Walhalla / 39
Tortoiseshell / 40
Squirrel / 41
Japanese Garden / 42

Return to Dreamtime
Flight SQ 235 / 45
Dreaming /46
Red Centre / 47
For Albert Namatjira / 48
Mount Sondar / 49
After Gold / 50
Black Swans / 51
Simpson's Gap / 52

No Cure in Tears and *Owlstone*
Taking down the Balloons / 55
For Christina Rossetti / 56
Crocuses / 57
Labels / 57
"As the sun dapples the water …" / 58
Branch Line / 59
Owlstone / 60
Elderberry '97 / 61
Abstract / 62
Axehead 63
Postcard of an Indian Ceremony / 64
Brumbies 1 and 2 / 65
Snowcry / 67
After Today's News / 68
Beyond Leathley / 69

NEW POEMS
Photographs on a pub wall / 73
PICTURES FROM AN OLD SUITCASE
Introduction / 74
World's End / 74
Twins / 75
Woman and man / 75
Airman in front of a pyramid / 76
Postcard of Singapore / 76
Young man standing at a studio table / 77

American Relations / 78
Beyond Cape Canaveral / 79
From the Frontier / 80
Isola Tiberina / 81
Capitoline / 82
Statuette / 83
Reflections / 83
On Shore Terminal / 84
Flamingos / 85
Hannah Noah speaks / 86
Oyster Woman / 87
VOICES OFF STAGE
Cook to the Capulets / 88
Drawing Master to Richard III / 89
Lady Macbeth's Sister / 90
Urban Foxes / 91
School Photos / 92
Peacock on a Library Roof / 93
Shadow Shapes / 94
Continuity / 95
The Grottoes of Catullus / 96
Sirmione / 98
War Cemetery / 99
Candles / 100
Just Another News Item / 101
The Night Café: Vincent Van Gogh 1888 / 102
Lupins / 103
Towton / 104

*For Mabel, Mary, Ken, Ian and Jo,
and all my friends with thanks
for their advice and encouragement.*

FOREWORD

THE BEST POETRY, like good apples and fine wine, keeps well. Pauline Kirk's poems yield fresh gifts on later readings and are always worth savouring. I have all her previous collections of poetry on my bookshelves so it is exciting to have a new volume from this author. *Walking to Snailbeach: Selected and New Poems* does not disappoint, and there are some fine new poems here as well as old friends, including the strong poem that gives this collection its title.

There is nothing flashy or esoteric about Pauline's consistently well-crafted work and its appeal is not only for poetry aficionados. She has always written accessible poems of great perception and because she has an excellent ear for the subtle ring and rhythm of words – without falling for the obvious – they are equally effective on the page or in performance.

In her new poems she has lost none of her old magic but seems to be widening her scope and speaking through different 'voices' – though each appreciably her own. She ventures into history and literature and even becomes the *Cook to the Capulets*. In *Lupins* she memorably uses the imagery of flowers to touch on the disturbing subject of child abuse. Cold winds blow through the lines of *From the Frontier,* which transports us to Hadrian's Wall and the loneliness of a Roman soldier writing home. *Just Another News Item,* a short, deceptively simple, poem takes us inside a courtroom we have all read about, presenting a chillingly vivid picture in a few lines. The last verse catches one by the throat: 'No doubt they thanked him. / apologised for being a nuisance. /How do those of us who remain / explain the inexplicable?" There is often humour in the author's writing and in *Hannah Noah Speaks* she takes a wry look at an old story from a contemporary angle.

Reading Pauline's words is like having cataracts removed from our inner eyes so that we perceive happenings and emotions with greater clarity of vision. She is a generous writer who celebrates the work of others, from The Brontes to Wordsworth. She ends her poem *For Christina Rossetti* 'our bleak midwinter has thawed my own.' She is the mistress of the last line.

Pauline Kirk is acute on relationships, with all the complexity of their rewards and difficulties, and though she is equally at home writing about urban or rural settings and moves comfortably across continents from Europe to Australia – I love some of her Australian poems, taken from *Return to Dreamtime* – she is essentially a very English poet. There will be places and people here you recognise. A delightful collection.

Mary Sheepshanks

Selected Poems
Scorpion Days and *Red Marl Brick*

SCORPION DAYS

"Quick," she called, and flattening their noses
like pink snails, her children stared.
Behind heated glass half a dozen scorpions lay,
spider legged and crab-clawed;
committee decisions
made after tea-break on Nature's holiday.

Small fingers rapped a challenge;
at once a tail coiled,
sand scattered in lethal lines and the children gasped,
afraid in a darkened hall.
Then I was alone and travelling in another hemisphere.

Once, amongst sand like broken brick, that same thrust
startled me, before vanishing beneath a burning stone.
I stood then as the children stood,
but without the security of glass,
a city dweller, crossing deserts of inexperience.
Now that scorpion was scuttling down the years, through
memories of theses and air-conditioned rooms.

Sensibly I smiled, breathed on a window,
drew brave circles or read cards explaining habitat.
Here our nasty things are tamed, spectator sports
shut in cages. Though somewhere in Australia
dangers run wild, we can walk softshoed.

Perhaps, but we have our days too,
when death waits with its sting curled.
We travel life like blue rinsed tourists
yet a sudden detour will leave us,
unprepared and afraid beside desert ways.
For those who love, a thousand terrors wait,
coiled beneath the stone.

WALKING TO SNAILBEACH

My past walked lanes like these,
Through fern and celandine
Seeking work. Small and blackened men,
They mined the coal from pit to pit,
Following change as a fly follows meat.
I am at home here.

Yet the images are strange, negative.
Along these hills a leaden white has hardened
Since Roman times; set into furnaces and roofs,
Ruins bleaching in fields barren of grass.
Here men shovelled stone
Or burrowed under a paradise of flower,
Ghost-white, destroying as they went.

Why do I know this place?
Some memory not my own calls me:
Ghosts of ancestors passing through.
I am not myself alone, but many,
A continuum, a rusting chain.
My links were forged between coal and cars
Among Black Country voices. Sweating women
Hammered my iron in backyard shops
(Brick bicycle sheds now); my beginnings are broken.

I have my legends of course,
Stories told me by ancient aunts
Knitting time in endless scarfs.
Greatgreatgrandmama
Bathed her husband in bread and milk
(His skin was stubborn to heal, burnt crisp
In a flashback.) Their son swam flooded stalls
And died. Somebody's cousin, brilliant with a piano,
Tried a career playing to the Movie Halls
The year Talkies came out.

I come from a long line of failures
But they changed a nation,
Walked from the Middle Ages into now,
Carrying a whole society.
In this silent place, amongst the spoil heaps
And columbine, my ghosts may stand with dignity.
Waiting my arrival, they watch,
White against white.

INHERITANCE

Greedily I scramble, careless of hawthorn or ditch,
snatching at Autumn's goods – eighty five pence
a punnet in the shops and sold to me
for the cost of a scratched hand and nettled legs.
Protected by ramparts of thorn, riches taunt:
jewels dusty with humanity, or sleek as Satan, whence,
legend says, they come, and return if left unpicked.
All are guarded by legions of spiders, who – spotted
like dalmations or yellow as wasps – tremble their webs,
their bodies shrivelled with cunning. My children
stand beside me, holding their plastic jugs, while I explain

which berries, though black as funerals are safe, and which,
Cuckoopint or Nightshade, though they flaunt
in red and purple beauty, offer only death.
My children listen as I too have listened,
learning a code that my mother also learnt,
title to an inheritance of wealth.
A lorry shatters past, and I start, suddenly
awed by that unbroken maternal line which links
some ancient Briton watching a scavenging bird,
to a busy lane, and my twentieth century self.

SLOW SPRING

Spring came slowly that first, bitter year,
The ash buds held in hard, black bands
Till June. Love hid itself, snow-smothered,
Yearning towards a southern town,
And friends laughing without me. Wearily
I shut my dreams, like the cabbage plants, in boxes,
Fearful of iron earth and frozen hands.

Now, two cold summers past,
The church is again etched on a steel sky
Between Picasso trees, yet love begins to grow,
Absurdly. The gardens are tracked only by foxes,
But for me green armies patrol their borders
And the heat of hyacinths burns a thaw.
I see with northern eyes now,
And winter is but an early spring.

ON SOUTHLAKE CRESCENT

With head bent against the noise of traffic,
She hurries by with her pram, thinking of illness
And boredom, and how to tempt a sick palate,
Till, beside her in the greenness
Of a privet hedge, she notices a spider's web.
So fragile and bejewelled a thing seeming
Strange amongst prefabs and parked cars,
She stops, and finds herself dreaming

Of another garden, where currant bushes
And laburnum grew. Then, moving closer,
She sees not one, but ten, twenty, webs in sheets
And whorls, arranged as if a demented
Spider had sought to impress a mate or simply
Gone berserk. Such profusion, flawlessly constructed,
Confuses her, until, not even hearing her baby cry,
She stands, lost in a wilderness of streets.

ALMOST A LOVE SONG

When I was young, love was served with spam
and hymn sandwiches – I thought it free
until warned by aunts in herbaceous hats.
Even love has its fee

they said, and passion offends the neighbours.
Like riding a bicycle in Oxfam sandals
it suits the arty sort, prone to scandals,
not a polite academic

like me. I have learnt wisdom now,
and yet, once every year or so my dear,
I need to tell you my gratitude
for past love and present care;

for tolerance when I have shouted,
or simply wanted to go, anywhere so long
as it was alone. I would burst into song,
like a new Ginger Rogers,

thrilling to my own Fred Astaire,
but the words I own will write a thesis,
not love. Dear, the thought is there;
you must write the song.

PARKINSON'S DISEASE

You were allotted six months' life, forty years ago,
But being the awkward sort, objected,
And, at a cost which I shall never know,
Death, and all such 'damn fools' rejected.
What you were then I have glimpsed from books
And 1920's snaps, or essays praised
By masters recognising intellect.
But today I see only what is left, as, beside me,
You try laboriously to collect,
Pushing with a fork till all is mushy,
Repellent. You drink and my child looks
How Grandad's hand shakes, the cup raised
By it splashing tea; then suddenly she presses
Two pink fists across her face and says,
"Grandad makes me feel sick. He messes."

I stop, embarrassed, and the silence flays
Your pain in weals across my mind.
Searing, it opens other sores gained when I too,
Child-unknowing, turned aside, shamed
On speechdays and boyfriends' visits by
You, Dad, as, shut in the prison of your head,
You shook hands and smiled, and tried to fulfil my
Expectation. "Don't be silly," I reprimand,
But not knowing how to atone to you,
My voice is unintentionally harsh, scolding
Past cruelty through her, till she unwraps her eyes
And avoiding your face, continues eating.
You of course say nothing, having forgiven worse –
The kindnesses that hide belief
That stammering implies deaf or daft, the relative
Who mocks incompetence in front of company –
Remembering these, I change the topic,
And in silent fury, sip my tea.

PLAGUE VILLAGE

Our schools study this place, write projects, or come on coaches
To view its church, the narrow streets, its stocks;
All Summer the cars arrive bringing after-dinner trippers;
They read the plaque and sigh before seeking antiques;
Eyam, plague village.

This Sunday a woman sits reading in a garden of roses
While passing crowds lean across her wall to seek the sign:
'Plague Cottages'. There – behind her – in those mellow houses
Deathly roses once bloomed, ring-a-ringing dying cheeks.
"George Viccars: September 7th. 1665."

Visitors gather round Mompesson's church,
Admire the ancient cross and loiter through the porch,
See his chair, and pause, gathering before an illumined page.
Sydall ... and Derby ... Hancock – Dear God, so many names ...
Eyam, plague village.

We leave for fresher air and stand amongst the flowers.
The trippers seek their coaches, beginning to chatter like sparrows,
Pleased with gifts and cards, pockets full of posies;
But we, being independent, stroll on past stone and roses,
Through a honied afternoon.

As directed, we raise a cover to observe a bull baiting ring,
Then, having eaten too much at lunch,
Decide on a green climbing path, through purple dead nettle
And wild white parsley, towards Mompesson's well, high above
Eyam, plague village.

An arrow directs us to a stone capped stream, where once goods
And food were left to aid a self-besieged community.
Afterwards I return alone, though with others, through woods
Those few survivors must have trudged.
Dear God, so many names ...

CRIPPLE SYKE

The names fascinate: 'Far Reef' and 'Bachelor'
'Poet's Corner', 'Low Fold' ...
The hill where the workhouse watches
boasts of being Troy, no less,
and this hard track they call 'Cripple Syke'.

Quietly I walk the ginnels, between walls older
than the houses they border. I love this place.
It gives a sense of continuity.
Gateposts cannibalised two centuries past
stand frozen, totems imprisoned

in stone. Across a busy road a horse shelters,
its mane braided by an aching wind.
I trace a mill pond in an oiled hollow,
find a stile left without a farm.
Slabs hewn by giants bridge an ancient stream;

drainpipes stain a darkening wall;
a weir whitens rock and weed.
Such scenes comfort me. Though red marl
and brick colour my childhood's dream,
not stone, I am at peace here.

My past and this past were made of the same iron;
the Black Country faces I recall
were drawn with the same harsh lines I see here:
the pinched look of cold, and work, and poverty.
I love this place. It is familiar to me.

EPIPHANY

We lean around white walls, good-humouredly
though a little moth-eaten, an average northern queue,
come on this bitter night to buy our feast.
Beyond an ancient fish-eyed window an unlucky few
still shiver, hoping to gain our heaven.
Cars flash between greystone homes

while Saturday night sylphs clack past,
the fine metal threads of their laughter
frayed by a wind sharp as a razor shell.
United by hunger, we enjoy the routine of waiting,
dislike the unexpected, the old lady whose tone
recalls a husband outranked only by death.

She fusses, insists she has lost a pound,
fumbles in her purse, and seeking our support,
looks round. Instead, we read notices or stare
along the road, as if seeing brothers home from sea.
"She never 'ad one," our chipshop Beatrice
confides, through an inferno of steam.

We smile as a small bewildered figure passes
beyond our view, still searching her purse.
Then suddenly we fall silent, each avoiding the other's eye.
We wonder if we too will grow confused, amusing ...
Staring through steam, we foresee journeys,
colder than a January sky.

MINER'S SONG: THE HORSFORTH BALLAD

(On February 5th 1806 the mouth of one of the bell pits in Horsforth collapsed, burying a number of miners alive. According to legend, they spoke for several days and air was admitted to them through a hole bored in the earth. Down this passage-way a few beans were scattered but no other relief could be given to the men, who remained underground for twelve days, until their bodies were brought to the surface.)

We were but poor men, used to cutting coal;
Not city ways. We trudged Lee Lane each day
With pick and boy, snap and stubborn mule.
Rough speech and hard work, 'twas the only way

We knew. We mined Lord Stanhope's land
And for Lord Stanhope's house and leisure
Crawled through clay and cold; a draggled band
Too weary for thoughts of Church or pleasure.

> O bury me in the green yard beside the church
> Or bury me at home near the buzzing hive;
> Bury me anywhere, sweet folk, moor or marsh,
> So long as you bury me not here, alive.

Bell pits are evil places, e'en seen in the sun.
They close on you sudden like, with a terror
Of falling soil and stone. We always feared this one,
Thought it time to move, but the maister

Said there was good coal to be won still
So we dug deeper, and sweated and swore
Though the wind blew coldly from off the hill.
By noon our throats were dry, our hands rubbed sore.

> O bury me in the green yard beside the church
> Or bury me at home near the buzzing hive;
> Bury me anywhere, sweet folk, moor or marsh,
> So long as you bury me not here, alive.

When the lad shouted his warning we ran too late;
There was nought we could do but scrabble
Like mice in a cage, sealed to our fate.
We were shut in together, a frightened rabble

Of eleven boys and men. A few of us prayed,
Most cursed Heaven or simply sat down and cried.
Then hope began. In time we would be saved,
Bob said, and honest Bob never lied.

> O bury me in the green yard beside the church
> Or bury me at home near the buzzing hive;
> Bury me anywhere, sweet folk, moor or marsh,
> So long as you bury me not here, alive.

They heard us tapping and calling at last,
And air was got to us for our prison was foul.
They dropped green beans for to break our fast,
But green beans will not stitch body to soul.

Now we are worn out with watching and waiting;
We dream of sunlight and hunting with dog and stave.
For near a week our women have stood watching,
But Lord Stanhope's field is like to be our grave.

> O bury me in the green yard beside the church
> Or bury me at home near the buzzing hive;
> Bury me anywhere, sweet folk, moor or marsh,
> So long as you bury me not here, alive.

NATIVITY PLAY

First come the angels, trailing clouds of bathroom net
and glory, tinsel bright under a cooking foil star.
Hitching white night-dresses above small white feet
they climb an unsteady heaven, and wave, towards earthly mothers.

Next comes Mary, immaculate in borrowed curtains,
while behind a piano a shuffling choir sings lul-ley
and Joseph forgets his lines. A doll is born,
explaining in two seconds a two thousand year mystery;

we smile, until nervous shepherds bring lambs
to give on cue, and we manage a carol or two,
four wheeler Christians singing an annual apology.
Then from classroom palaces, kings appear.

They offer tea caddies and myrrh in a biscuit tin
but my thoughts have left them, travelling private deserts
to sit in a hospital ward, beside a dignified, dying man.
Returning, I find a troop of grenadiers in crepe paper,

each tapping my grief on a sweet nostalgic drum.
"Tar-rump-pap-pum-pum" they play, "What shall I give him?
Ta-rump-pap-pum-pum ..." This Christmas the holly pricks –
my gift must be a loved old man.

TURTLES

Each Spring a gentle tide floods a distant sand:
baby turtles creeping to a sharp beaked death.
In Summer gentle mouselike things scurry our land
prey to eyes as bright as the winter moon. The earth

is not the place we would pretend. We call Nature kind,
forgetting how a million lives float helplessly,
drowned in its wastefulness, its beautiful blind
plenty. The starlings squabbling on our lawn endlessly

warn us, with their funeral dress and assassin's eye;
the fox prowling a chicken run at grey dawn,
the swallow's exultant swoop through a quivering sky ...
Our own days began in a frenzied swim of spawn;

we threshed our way to life, howling to survive,
yet still we feel surprise when we turn a rotten tree
or find a rabbit's carcass alive with breeding,
buzzing flies. Nature's cruel beauty

troubles us, will not fit our dreams of lambs and flowers.
We turn away and shudder. Yet in the hot night
of our suburban minds beauty still glowers,
waits for us in thickets of memory, tiger bright.

MUTTONBIRDS*

They came at dusk, in a rhythm of wings
We sensed but could not see –
Though we peered till our necks jammed.
Beyond us crowds lined the night's penguin parade,
But being lovers we had chosen a side-show
And waited, a battered car our hide.
Suddenly instinct became form:
A dark shape approaching, between sky and sea.

One, then ten, a hundred
Beating flapping things passed us,
Oblivious of our presence though shot and snared
Towards extinction. Amazed by such silent movement
We watched, until, recalling a Dreamtime
When a million muttonbirds returned to land
Each night, we could not speak, but sat,
Absorbed in sky and sea.

That night was five thousand miles ago
And we are richer, busier now,
Riding a rollercoaster down to death.
Once we heard muttonbirds touch the sand
But we have so little silence now.
Dear, our hopes shorten and our quarrels lengthen.
Let us be still again and love,
Before we too pass, like the muttonbirds,
Scattered between sky and sea.

* Muttonbirds: large seabirds found along the coast of Victoria, Australia.

Rights of Way and *Travelling Solo*

CELEBRATION

Our shapes are dark,
Halloweens against orange flame.
We stamp in boots, bang gloved hands
and await the firework display.
We have paid a pound to freeze thus.
The hot dogs steam for charity.

Below us the streets are dark,
but on other hills other bonfires blaze,
each dedicated to a rebellion
barely remembered. Long before,
when this school field was heath,
it was Samhain we celebrated.

Then the whole land was dark
and the dead warmed their hands
beside us. Romans marched the valleys
and each rock and tree had meaning.
We burnt more than a doll then –
our gods were feared, not played at.

Now we gasp as rockets are lit
but the faces upturned are Celtic still.
For two thousand years the bonfires
have burned, and the dance stirs our feet
even now. Once more the old ring joins,
unconsciously.

DECEMBER

The horizon has been stolen by night.
Ships swing on a blackened sky.

We walk the empty promenade
Companionship wrapped about our ears.

Below us, a dog barks in sharp delight;
The sea is velvet trimmed with lace.

Close for warmth and out of habit
We talk of men and mice, put worlds to right

While along the bay the funfair flares,
And posters promise end of season thrills.

We pass Georgian porches lit with palms;
A room is red and gold, set for dinner.

Come nearer, dear. The night grows cold.
Let us shelter here beyond the yellow glare

Of other people's busyness. See my dear –
How our breath hangs before us.

BRONTË BRIDGE

So this is the place:
Stone slabs laid over a stream
And a trickle of water cutting a hillside –
Better when the snowmelts tumble no doubt
But pretty enough and cold on unbooted feet.

To this place the children came,
Charlotte, Emily, Branwell and Anne,
Living their wild life in imagination,
Thrown in on each other's company,
Thought a bit queer by local folk.

To this place also Charlotte walked,
Pregnant and alone when the rest were dead.
She did not long survive that last visit.
Now signs mark the route she took
And Sunday strollers make their pilgrimage.

They find it further than expected,
Wish for flatter shoes, struggle with buggies.
Children splash and squeal in the water
While a girl sits, plugged to synthetic sound.
She does not hear the water's soft conversation.

Yet in our different ways we each pay homage,
If only with unaccustomed effort,
Leaving cars and ice-cream vans behind.
Charlotte, Emily, Branwell and Anne,
We remember you.

MISS TEMPLETON

"Poor Miss Templeton"
the neighbours said, smiling
despite their good intentions.
With her chatter of weddings and suitors
she was quite a turn, to outsiders.

Coquetry did not become her.
It clashed with academic stoop
and sensible shoes. On the wall
above photos of sisters – long dead –
a Diploma proved the Templeton claim

to fame and a modest livelihood.
She who had accompanied
the great Mr Tubb (such a lovely tenor)
and taught a thousand hopeful Chopins
had no reason to flirt and simper.

Still, as the Home Help said,
chopping potatoes like traitors' heads,
age and loss of hope and youth
and a deficiency of oxygen to the brain
may make Miss Templetons of us all.

There the laughter stopped. Truth,
like cucumber, sits uneasily
on nervous stomachs. For Miss Templeton
the nightmare goes on, and she winks
as she sits, all Reason gone.

NAILHOUSE

My people made nails like these,
beaten sharp, cut from the rod.
These shears and bellows
are the sort they once used.
The museum grate is filled with paper
but some sense of toil touches us:
the tiny window, the rotten door.

In a nailhouse like this, six by four,
Greatgrandmama kept her children fed.
Being widowed she had little choice,
and her mother, widowed too and aged,
had less. So they sweated together
and sang their hymns. In Summer
they would have stripped to the waist.
The children worked too; their play
was sweeping and packing; blowing bellows.

The cottages are desirable today;
plant pots sit on nailhouse windows.
The young favour homes with character
so long as they have baths and videos.
History is marketable now.
For Greatgrandmama, History was sweat
and a widow's bag of nails.

FAITH TEA

"Faith Tea this Saturday.
Speaker Miss Ivy Harbottle."
Driving past the sign I smiled.
Do they still have Faith Teas?

All the way down the road
I was getting ready for tea and faith,
with a bow in my hair big enough
for wings, and Dad fastening his cuffs,
while the gasfire spluttered and the cat
swung on Mum's corset laces.
Spirella did well in those days,
before ladies let it all hang out.

Those were simpler times,
or so they seem now.
We used to walk into the chapel
knowing why we were there: for faith
and angel cakes, both thought good
for building you up. Now cakes
are suspect, being high in cholesterol,
and faith is circumspect, admitted
only between consenting adults.

Would I return to those days?
A simpler past has its attraction
viewed from a morning traffic jam,
and I have almost forgotten
the piano was off key and the buns,
like the ladies who served them,
ample but of undetermined age.
Still, I doubt if I'd settle.
My life has sprawled too much
to cram into a simple faith,
or a girdle.

MARSDEN MEMORIAL

In Horsforth, Yorkshire, there is a plaque which states:
*"The Reverend Samuel Marsden 1764-1838, Christian
Missionary and pioneer of the wool producing industry
in Australia and New Zealand, served as an apprentice
in a smithy near this place."*

Near this garden a hero served apprentice,
Hammered nails and sweated in his uncle's pay.
A plaque and ancient anvil rank him pioneer,
Recall the woollen trade. Strange to think this smithy,
These weeds and litter are sacred, part of history.
With pride Horsforth claims its missionary.
Forge and eucalypt unite, bind youth to adult fame.

Like Samuel I also served apprentice,
But in that land where first he took men and sheep.
I learnt an academic trade in rooms hot as any forge,
Read his penal code. He was thought no hero there:
Judged harsh, official, forger of iron rules,
A jailor's chaplain, hammering souls.
He bore the taint of Botany Bay, the long nails

Beaten into minds, the term of natural life.
His colony served as dump for England's waste,
Thieves, prostitutes, not many innocent.
There is always the other story. Those sheep he took,
Valued more than men cramming a fevered hold,
Fattened on stolen land. And here in Yorkshire cold,
Where their fleeces were washed, woven, sold,

There was curse as well as wage for those
Who flocked from villages, into blackened folds.
Beside the anvil I recall another place, another view.
I wonder, in that land of bell birds, did Samuel find
Memory visiting this English scene? Did his mind
Hammer horseshoes? Forge and eucalypt unite, bind
Truth to truth, youth to adult fame.

REQUIEM FOR AN ENEMY

When the affair started,
I could scarcely think who you were:
a woman met at a poetry reading,
rather drunk, colour of eyes not recalled.
Then my telephone line
became umbilical cord to a viper.
I learnt to hate you.
Later, your apology touched me.
After all, to admit blame is
more than most politicians manage,
and I did understand – a little.
Jealousy is a pain I too have felt.

This year, I heard of your death.
Though I was sorry for an hour or two,
mostly I forgot you.
Now, amongst a file of proofs
brought to speed a train,
I find this poem.
Your life space is written beneath.
Suddenly, I can read no more.
I must turn to my window and look out,
lest the watching eyes begin to stare.
How could you create such beauty
when, for me, words are dark, secretive,
found only after weeks of searching?

My scarcely-known enemy,
it is I who must envy you.

OUTBREAK OF WAR

My day passes with the scent of cake.
I break an egg into a well of flour
and listen as the radio states:
"Last ditch attempt at peace."
Next Tuesday, war may begin.
Experts talk of pre-emptive strikes;
I line and grease a baking tray.

If asked, I would warn
that skin, like eggshell, is thin
and will smash when struck by steel.
No one seeks my opinion,
though they may well require my son.
So, folding currants into yellow paste,
I watch them sink, like soldiers into sand.

Work must be done, whatever the news.
The labourer tilled his field
while Napoleon camped beyond his hedge.
As Anthony and Cleopatra fought,
their slaves went on chiselling.
Tomorrow, I shall buy extra bread,
and candles, in case the lights go out.

REFUGEES

When do we leave –
Cancel the milk, stop the papers?
There are whispers on the train
And letters go astray.
We are not wanted here.

Once, we were decent folk,
Growing a little stout,
Respecting the law and the neighbours.
We cast our vote, when we remembered,
And forgot it decently afterwards.

Now waiters refuse to serve us
And the school has no places.
The man on the street shouts hate
Not news, and our parties are invaded
By black-shirted men.

Perhaps we should pack our cases.
But where should we go? And how?
The wind blows cold across the station.
Who would want us, anyway –
Decent folk, growing a little stout?

WALHALLA

When I first drove past this town,
a thicket of graves sprawled uphill
Cleopatra's needles, urns in shrouds,
tasteful cherubim.
Each local stalwart had bought respect,
been done with ham and polished scrolls –
Myers, and Marsden, Blythe, Gledhill ...

Now three obelisks stand alone,
sole survivors in a forest of beech.
Coal Hill Cemetery is almost rural.
Five years ago, nothing predicted
such suffocation. I recall
a few saplings – birch and elder –
but no threat to Yorkshire stone.

Amongst my souvenirs are photos,
taken in another such forgotten place,
where men mined gold, and grew so sure,
that they named their town Walhalla.
We found its cricket ground, a flatter space
traced through Bush, but shops, bars,
crowds were smothered in eucalypt.

So many hopes, so many deaths,
all to be lost in scrub.
I begin to fear a world
suffocated in eucalypt and elder;
and Paris, London, Canberra,
no more than flatter spaces,
half-way up a windy hill.

TORTOISESHELL

A splash of June in a February church;
you soar to the rafters,
then flutter against the window pane.
I fear for your safety.
Try as I will, I cannot concentrate,
but must watch your patterning.
How did you first arrive?
Were you trapped in flesh,
brought by some behatted lady
arranging flowers on a pulpit ledge?

If I were a medieval peasant –
or a TV evangelist – I would think
you were sent by the Devil to distract me.
You call me to another decade
and a ward sister's office,
two beds from my father's dying.
"Look!" Sister said, surprising us both.
"There's a butterfly on your dress!"
I wanted to talk of comas and chances.
She talked of butterflies.

At the time, I thought her heartless.
Now I hear the pleasure in her voice.
A nurse sees death many times,
but such unexpected beauty rarely.
Sitting in my pew, I consider
both butterfly and father anew.
Though your body was slight
and the odds stacked by illness,
you no more admitted defeat
than this out-of-season tortoiseshell.

Forgive me. Your courage
had faded from my mind. Today
it has clarity again.

SQUIRREL

Frozen by fear and car headlights,
You come to depend upon me,
Interfere with my plans. You have rights:
I cannot callously drive over you.

I must move you, it seems, bodily.
Half-vexed, half-amused, I leave my car,
Though the lane is lonely
And time pressing.

Your heart beats under my hand:
Your warmth surprises, reminds me
Of kittens and piglets and days on the land.
Apologising, I place you on a wall.

Suddenly, you find life. Your back arches,
Then you vanish into dusk.
For a moment, my city self pauses,
Envying the wild. All that evening,
Your heart beats on, under my hand.

JAPANESE GARDEN

This mud was meant to be a garden.
School children planted trees;
youths on a Government scheme
arranged rocks,
laid out sand.
Now the pond is thick with ice,
the bridges are broken.
What vandals did not destroy,
our climate has contorted.

There is tranquillity here, even so.
The carp stone rises to Heaven;
beauty hovers between frozen reeds
and Winter sun. Beyond the fence,
a hockey whistle blows,
but here there is rest.
My feet crunch ice.
From the hawthorn,
a robin lifts in silent flight.

The Japanese were a warlike people,
yet they preserved such places.
Their Samurai must have stood,
as I stand now, thinking of time:
the burning days,
the peasant lugging his life.
Through the lines of rock and water,
they saw the eternal, and found relief.
Briefly, I share their peace.

Return to Dreamtime

FLIGHT SQ235

When I was a child, I used to trap
infinity in a dressing table mirror.
Carefully arranged, the hinged panels

would reflect one into another
until my image retreated
down avenues of faces, all of them

mine. It was a favourite game,
more piquant for being vanity
indulged in a forbidden room.

Tonight it is only my eyes that reflect.
Distorted by port hole glass,
they split into two dozen lids and pupils.

Blurred like my spirit, they are pools
drawing me into an unseeing night.
Nothing exists beyond myself –

no cloud or moon or curve of earth.
Sleep clogs the narrow air.
Bodies slump in unfriendly seats.

My mind insists that coast and sea
lie beneath, but my eyes report
only infinity.

DREAMING

Nowadays I dream little –
of corridors I must walk endlessly
or the odd exam nightmare
with two years' work to revise in a night.
While I was a girl, whole cities burnt in my brain;
waves pounded my room. God was a Puritan
and reared in Black Country chapels.
I never had the courage to sin.
Judgement Day was too real a setting
to risk in my dreams.

At twenty, I had to clear the Old Tyrant out,
though I kept His charismatic son.
Hell became merely a coach ride to Rhyl
with sing-along favourites all the way.
If I thought of Heaven at all, it was a queue
for my book-signing right round the block.
My longings are in this life: for friendship and love,
warmth and width of sky. For a while I found
such rarities here. This land is my legend;
my Dreamtime and youth in one.

RED CENTRE

Below us, the Outback unfolds:
parched river beds meander,
grey-green through yellowing hills.
Then the real desert begins.
Warm and red and deadly, it waits,
beneath derisory clouds.
A never-ending horizon moves before us.

Seen through the safety of toughened glass,
the red heart throbs with heat.
Broken veins of river bed cross
and recross; capillaries of creek
thread aimlessly. Nothing moves,
except us. Our wings shadow
long straight tracks, leading nowhere.

I feel as if I am returning home,
yet I have crossed this land once
only, long ago. Whole expeditions
have vanished among those sands –
so why do I long to be below,
not safely strapped above, cutting
my plastic food with plastic knife and fork?

FOR ALBERT NAMATJIRA:
ABORIGINAL ARTIST (1902-1959)

The ghost gums are not as he painted.
Beyond them, the view is still blue and ochre,
The hills a purple wash through heat,
But the trees he loved are dying,
Heart gone, like himself.

His memorial stands vandalised.
Once it recalled an artist imprisoned
For observing tribal custom. He shared –
As Family do – and gave alcohol
To mission station blacks, ignoring statute.

Red ants ate his wooden tribute whole,
So local friends tried brass, and got bored
With replacing stolen plaques. Now nothing
Marks Albert's favourite place, except a view
And two gaunt eucalypts.

As we rejoin our air-conditioned coach
We find such continuing anger odd. Surely
It was enough to deny him ancestral land,
To confine him to mission school and alien law,
Ban him from living in his nearest town?

Still, we are outsiders and do not know the fear
That a man we termed 'Abo' and 'Primitive'
Could outpaint us with every stroke –
And in Western style too.
Ghost gums, you are memorial enough.

MOUNT SONDAR

We can see her clearly now:
A pregnant *lubra** in profile. Breasts full,
stomach swollen with child, she fills
our horizon. Her navel is distended,
the left nipple raised, hard and ready.
Mountain mother, she rests,
before the crisis of birth.
This land is full of such strange images.
A ridge of sandstone is a lizard's spine,
that dry creek, the mark of the snake.

Later, we drink beer in a high-class hotel,
near a dried-out river in a drier gorge
some homesick pioneer misnamed
Glen Helen. A heron skims above sand
so hot we must close our eyes.
Next door, a wedding babbles.
The bride giggles and blows her veil.
Once an orchestra performed here,
chairs and cellos stuck in gravel.

We walk beneath a polished sky
and find a waterhole full of tiny fish.
The sand around it sears our feet.
Given rain up river, the Finke
could roar again, sweeping through
hotel and bar and petrol pump.
It has happened before.
The mountain mother would barely stir,
having heard such things many times,
Generation to generation.

*Aboriginal woman

AFTER GOLD

Nothing will grow here, not even the sour grass
that soothes neglected paddocks. In their haste,
men tore a valley inside out, spewed gravel
on to startled fields. Each knew of fortunes made
by others, of nuggets of gold, big as a fist.
Most were lucky to scrape enough dust
to buy next week's tucker, or medicines
for rotting feet and chest.

I grew up in other such blighted places,
among moonscapes of ash, red marl holes,
quarries weeping fern. Great-great-grandpapa
mined black gold across four counties
and saw the coal pits die, one by one.
He made no fortune. Dig in the new estates
round Dudley and you'll find my inheritance.
The soil is grey; lawns grow poorly still.

Gold or tin, coal, copper, it was all the same
to the miner, a commodity to be seized,
in risk and damp and shortening breath.
Neither Great-great-grandad nor gold digger
had time to think how the land bled,
how long it takes scabs of grass to form.
How could they fight a philosophy
that valued them as commodity too?

BLACK SWANS

Most English parks have one now:
a token exotic swimming unhappily,
just beyond the Sunday Outing lawns.
When the Pioneers saw their first black swans,
they thought them weird, born of a land where
trees shed bark, not leaves, and magpies carol prettily.

The shock of the new is gone for us, but seen
where they belong, the grace of these dark spirits
still amazes. Their reflections shadow the shadows,
recall tales of charmed princes, gliding their life away.
In the Dreaming, they are the Baimul, brothers
turned to swans, and from white to black.

The legend is as dark as any Celtic myth.
It tells how Warunna, the clever one,
changed his kin to birds, to distract the Wi-bulloo –
spirit women – and gain weapons unseen by man.
Forgetting his brothers, he set off for Oobi-Oobi,
the sacred mountain, the Baimul calling behind him.

Eaglehawks fell upon them and carried them away.
They tore out the Baimul's feathers, leaving the birds
bleeding and cold, until crows took pity and gave
their feathers to keep them warm. Warrunna knew his kin,
but he had dared to visit Baiame's sky camp before his time.
His power had gone. He could not change them back.

That is why Southern swans are black, the legend says,
except for a few white tail feathers, and the down next
to their skin. It is also why their beaks are red as blood.
Today we are reminded of that dark side of beauty.
A small dog's bark turns elegance to spitting rage.
The swans attack. Picnickers and tourists flee.

SIMPSON'S GAP

At first, this place disappoints, bitterly.
There is a metalled road now,
A coach turning bay. Man-made steps
Lead to brackish pools and a darkening cleft.

I recall virgin sand and ochre;
Sun pouring down on water –
Perfection; not a nature reserve
Tidied up for tourists.

Dusk settles. Suddenly among the rocks
A bell rings, clearer than glass. It calls
Like hope on frosty nights, song in marble halls.
Startled, we look round, not sure

Whether to seek bird or man.
Again and again, the bell song rings,
Indescribable; beauty
To hold in the memory.

The music of ancestral souls steals my spirit.
Its magic paints scrub and spinifex.
Yet the only movement is slight:
A small bird flitting through fading light.

So pure a sound belies its dowdy clothes.
It must come from brighter species, surely,
with splendid wings and golden mouth?
My throat tightens. I am glad I came.

No Cure in Tears and *Owlstone*

TAKING DOWN THE BALLOONS

We fetch a ladder and climb,
taking down the balloons.
Red and blue, yellow and green,
their colours float about the room
as clear as childhood dreams.
'Birthday Boy', 'Twenty-one Today' ...
balloons mark our celebrations,
our rites of passage:
another Christmas spent,
a son grown, a daughter flown.

We would preserve our joys on strings
but the moments deflate,
shrink around our fingers.
There is sadness in empty glasses,
you say, and torn balloons look untidy.
The son will leave, the daughter marry.
True, my Love. I would grieve too,
But each taking down
marks a beginning,
not just an ending.

Hear how Time's music plays!
The conga of life dances on,
carrying us to other rooms,
other celebrations.
It leaves no pause for mourning
and we dance so well together.
Let me fill your glass again.
We will put up more balloons,
red ones for our love,
bright yellow for our future.

FOR CHRISTINA ROSSETTI

We have no snow upon snow this year,
Just wind and rain and a blackened river.
In your day Midwinter was bleaker,
Before power stations and cars.
Yet your childhood sounds warmer than ours.
A gaiety of visiting émigrés heated your parlour;
You talked poetry with Grandfather Polidori,
Lent your face to brother Dante's art. No wonder
Your head hummed with singing birds and sprites.

I would not change with you, even so.
Only men could gain brotherhood of arts then,
However Pre-Raphaelite.
You were taught to come second, posed as virgin
Until you could play no other part.
Faith knitted you a thin comforter and you did your duty,
Cared for mother and aunts, hid your body in bombazine.
By the time cancer beat you, you must have wondered
If life was worth your song.

A hundred years on, two galleries are full of you.
Your features cover their walls.
As I walk into a London Winter, my mind
Sings your rhythms, your carols lift my soul.
Despite our differering times, we share so much:
A woman's conscience, mother, aunts ...
Too little time for creation.
Suddenly, in my head, I am writing again.
After eight months' silence words bang at my brain.

Watching Christmas lights plait along the river,
I thank you, Christina, woman to woman.
Your bleak Midwinter has thawed my own.

CROCUSES

Despair crouched, like a gargoyle
at the corner of her mind,
soot clothed, fingers to mouth.

An April northerly had moaned
all night, bending the trees,
blighting hopes like seeds.

Then suddenly on a verge
where mud and ice seeped
still, there was joy, blowing.

Crocuses:
purple and yellow,
an ambush of delight.

LABELS

They were put on firmly – stuff goes walk-about
in a Home like this. Now the name tags come off
in bits; like my memories of you.

Clearing out your clothes, I remember
where each was bought, the slippers we hunted for,
the dress that we guessed for size.

I test pens, throwing out the ones that won't write.
Left unused, ink soon dries – like personality,
speech, intellect.

Then I find your photos, neatly folded in polythene,
fragments of life, to catch me unawares,
and lacerate my calm.

Cruellest of all, though, are these torn strips of name.
They leave a smear of loss on all my inheritance.
Their stain will trouble me for years to come.

"AS THE SUN DAPPLES THE WATER ..."

The catalogue talks of reed-fringed rivers,
of wide open skies, wind pumps and flowers.
It claims snipe and lapwing, even bittern.
Shiny pages portray pubs or museums,
and boats, so many boats.
The waters lap through grass and sedge.

A Danish king settled here and left his name;
wool-merchants their wealth and churches, a remote
and enigmatic place, religiously drained. Their houses
are hotels now; the staithes where reeds were loaded
harbour other boats – so many boats.
The waters seep through grass and sedge.

Tourists have found this haven. They come
in their thousands, seeking the tranquillity
denied at home. Skipper and Matelot, Cruiseliner,
Kingfishers without wings, each shreds the peace
it seeks – Boats, so many boats.
The waters surge through grass and sedge.

*"A continual programme of upgrading
ensures all our boats have Colour TV, quality matching
china and portable phone ..."* Comfort is assured,
for wide skies can chill, and starlight perturb those
more used to florescent strip. Boats, so many boats.
The waters rush through grass and sedge.

We begin to wear away what we love.
The bittern is almost silent. Nature Reserves
must preserve what was once common currency.
Yet who would deny the city dweller their two weeks
of longed-for peace – or their boats, though
their passage tears through grass and sedge?

BRANCH LINE

They have marched pylons across my youth,
built raw red estates down my memories.
I do not know this place; image and truth
have parted. I hear Black Country voices
and notice my educated tone. From my dirty train
I recognise banks and paths I used to run
and afterthoughts of familiar streets remain,
yet the view is new to me. Drawn by February sun
bookend flats cover yards once crisp with washing,
or shadow parlours where curtains twitch curiously.
Though I recall oases of green and thrushes calling,
concrete has gained supremacy.

Only the names are familiar, their letters peeling fast,
fading from signs on Victorian stations. Lye ...
Langley Green, where my schooldays snickered past ...
Cradley Heath: names recalling Family,
associated with fat great aunts and extra chapel.
Pigeon lofts still whiten sky and grass;
mattresses spring on dumps as usual
and ragwort grows yet amongst broken glass,
but the land of my childhood is changed.
I watch the names flicker beside me
and check my map. The nymphs are departed;
the loitering schoolgirls are grown, irrevocably.

OWLSTONE

Drawn by polished stone,
I bend toward seaweed and flies,
and find you. Your rings and whorls
fascinate, remind me of the clinker
of my youth: man-made lava, paving
Black-Country tracks I used to walk,
with torch and freezing hands.

Granite, shale, igneous – my untutored eye
cannot distinguish. To me you are simply
an owl. Two rings of eyes peer at me,
above a crooked beak, cruel but wise.
What baleful witch imprisoned you?
Did you know too much – see histories
so secret they froze you into stone?

When we first came to this house, owls
greeted us. They would pause in our tree
and hoot, frightening sleep.
Now both tree and owls are gone.
Owls flew in my childhood too,
flapping through dreams, while I shivered
in a tent between apple trees.

Owls no longer watch from Wyre Hill.
The orchards are semi-detached now,
too regimented for flight –
like my life. Owlstone,
you must preserve their spirit for me,
sealed in stone, a curiosity
to remind me of the Wild I have lost.

ELDERBERRY '97

Writing out the label, I pause,
recalling a narrow track and berries in '97.
A witch of old in my kitchen,
I siphon Summers into demijohns.
That July was good for strawberries,
this a sour one, needing extra sugar.

Suddenly, in a saucepan lid,
I see my grandmother's face,
distorted above a flowered pinnie.
"Try my dandelion," she insists,
and, salving her Methodist guilt,
adds, "It's home-made – not alcoholic."

Not alcoholic!
A glass of Granny's dandelion
would unfreeze a politician's hand.
Her elderflower made our Christmas carols
twice as jolly. Gran's arts were needed, too,
with a gale off the lane and under her door.

Sometimes, though, her magic was too strong.
On hot nights, corks would pop in the scullery,
setting us laughing in fright, while wine ran
like revolutionary hordes towards us.
I wonder how Gran would judge me now?
She would scorn my new-fangled gadgets,

having never fathomed a vacuum cleaner;
consider my central heating soft
and my education beyond my station.
Still, I think she would smile
and pass me a glass of her elderberry,
one witch to another.

ABSTRACT

"Don't climb on the statue!"
The teacher's voice chills my afternoon.
"Come along children! Time's getting on."
Her class gathers, while I watch,
eating sandwiches. Near us, the giant bell

gapes, inviting small boys and irregular poets.
We could crawl together, into the mouth
and slide bumpily down, on our bottoms.
You would hear my whoops
right across the Sculpture Park.

What's it do, Miss?" a voice demands.
Teacher pauses. "It's a giant pod," she says,
"Something from Nature. Come off at once!"
"Please don't climb on the statue," a notice asks,
more politely. Then why make such a slidey,

slithery shape, metal on metal,
a perfect climbing frame?
I'll bet the squirrels ignore such signs,
after hours. Furtively a straggler
darts back and takes a surreptitious slither.

Being less athletic I slide my hand,
and wonder about the tyranny of taste.
How do you create such perfection,
knowing your audience will still ask,
"But what does it *do* ...?"

AXE HEAD

My palm cups carefully,
around an edge still sharp
after how many years? –
a millennium or two, three perhaps.
The haft vanished long ago,
wood being more human,
soon rotted. But this flint lasted,
dropped on a hillside, to be found
and dropped again over centuries,
thought no more than an odd-shaped stone.

Now I examine workmanship
I cannot emulate.
Put me in our cold, hostile History
without my car and supermarket,
and I would be lost, starving.
With your subtle shades of grey,
your flaked, chipped edge,
you link me to ancestors we call
primitive, yet whose skills we may need
one endless, nuclear winter ahead.

POSTCARD OF AN INDIAN CEREMONY

Dry hills and open plains,
harsh sky watching;
rock warm in the afternoon,
roads linking to Heaven.

We stand waiting our future:
the god who reveals all.
He comes by boat unseen
but known, red and gold.

Many sided, many faced,
Lord Shivah teach us.
Carry our sorrows.
Hear us; bless us.

We, the young, worship.
We wait, earth bound
among dry plains, under
drier skies – watching.

BRUMBIES

I

Wild horses thundered beside my bed last night
their hooves striking stones beneath my spine.
Peering under a torn flap in memory's tent
I looked out and saw darkness, more tangible than light.
A desert cold surrounded me, stars poured like wine
above me, and I smelt once more the wild red scent
of horse and scrub. Like sand from an unstable height
My soul flowed to another place, another time.
Today I travel on buses, am conscientious,
claimed by duty. In life's footnotes I am cited
politely, and though thought sharp about my edges
am seen as reliable, all my travels mortgaged,
husbanded, childed. They little know me.
Through my mind wild horses pass, across a desert sea.

II

They are shooting the wild horses of Australia;
crouched near a billabong or by ghostgum trees,
in the close red dark of a desert night,
the marksmen wait.
Drinking coke or checking tyres and rifles
the white men spit and think of money,
grow impatient, cast thin shadows on dust and scrub.
Beside them the hired aborigines sit,
having learnt how best to wait
a thousand thousand years ago.

They are shooting the wild horses of Australia,
meeting the requirements of today's market,
the American dealers, the Argentine exporters,
so careful of disease, so thoughtful of profit.
The wild horses must go, their end was decided;
cattle barons voted, secretaries typed minutes.
A BBC announcer proclaimed it.
All meat must be inspected,
kept free of the wild, the wandering herds that travel
uninvited throughout a desert night.

They are shooting the wild horses of Australia;
hearing the news reader's voice
I recall our own red desert night,
so dark we held the hours in our outstretched hands.
Beyond a canvas wall brumbies passed,
their hooves shaking the dust beneath our heads.
Next morning, in love with the wild and each other,
we stared in wonder at the shoeless prints,
the lines of churned up dust and scrub,
the scattered stones, still smelling of horse.

They are shooting the wild horses of Australia.
All through my dreams the brumbies die.
They lift their black heads in surprise,
begin to gallop, thunder ahead of the landrover,
eyes wide, nostrils dilated.
Suddenly one leaps, snaps its black back
and falls, whinnying against the moon.
The scattered stones still smell of horse.

I cannot watch. My eyes dazzle,
though I am thirty thousand miles away.

SNOW CRY

The polar bear's chest breasts the water,
White matted fur, ice drops glistening.
I hear music of winter, crunching, glinting,
Baying on night winds, night wolves neighing.
Hold me. Warm me. The wind blows cold.
My muscles tighten – old, old.

Still the polar bear waits, eyes in fur.
Watching through ice, it scents my skin.
My thin voice calls, slight through wind.
Dear – can you hear? Fold me, keep me,
Warm my hands in yours.
The cold stiffens, my fingers go taut.

I call and you unlock me.
Then you let go, leaving me bereft.
Hold me, keep me, or I shall drift,
Sleepless on snow like the sky above.
I have no furs, only thin cotton,
And the day grows dark and grey.
Silently white bears watch me, cold-eyed on ice.

AFTER TODAY'S NEWS

After today's news, everything is sharper,
Brighter, more beautiful.
There are daffodils opening in my mind.
Their leaves sting my eyes.

Ahead, lovers are standing on a bridge.
I notice how they move, the gesture
Of her hand. Roofed with night,
the abbey stalks the moon.

I should miss such things.
I had grown used to this world's joy,
But now my sight is amazed, hurts
With the loveliness of life.

Was this how it felt, Milton?
The surprise, not quite believing,
Seeing everything with new eyes,
Knowing you might be losing the old?

BEYOND LEATHLEY

This is not Top Withens, nor any such literary place,
but an unnamed farm that raised a stubborn face
towards sullen land and obstinate fields.

Now lintels hewn by giants frame a broken sky;
balance door shafts in Georgian symmetry
A courtyard shines through grass –

we walk it down a crystal afternoon.
Pheasants rasp like rusty gates, and a shred of moon
surprises. Slowly the land becomes softer.

Celandines splash light; a milky way of wood aven
glows beside a stream. Yet even in this quiet haven
winter debris strews the scene. Branches

breed monsters; whole trees lie, roots clamped
in clay. Two hundred years of growth ended
in one February storm, yet today that same wind

offers life. I gulp its gift, forgetting the afternoons
lost to darkness, the eternity of mud-soaked March.
Like the celandines, I turn towards the sun, and open.

New Work

PHOTOGRAPHS ON A PUB WALL

Eyes framed in gilded wood
criticise my evening drink.
A woman in hunting gear poses;
carters smoke reflective pipes.
Centre space on the far wall
(above the immitation fireplace)
a couple prepares to picnic,
bottle of wine and glasses
propped on a rickety stool.
Who were you all?

What lives, dreams,
lay behind each image,
caught for posterity
and to decorate a noisy pub?
No one answers my question
though a parade of beauty queens
stares back, unexplained.
Lord, let me not end so,
my life sold on a market stall –
pub decor to another age.

PICTURES FROM AN OLD SUITCASE

There must be hundreds:
box brownie, kodachrome snap,
postcard, in memoriam.
Stuffed together without time
or logic, the debris of two lives
crammed in an old suitcase.

Running out of excuses,
I begin the long-vowed 'sorting out',
braving the dust of memory.
Sharp corners of emotion
catch my fingers,
remind me of places and people
I know, but do not recognise ....

*

World's End

This was Country
– or what had once been such.
A few stray cows lingered still,
while scrubby hawthorn whitened hedges
beside motor cycle tracks.
We walked to World's End each Sunday,
crossing the main road, and beyond,
past safe suburban boxes,
towards an odd little chapel
until today I had forgotten.
For a year or more it drew my parents
– peripatetic worshippers, always moving on,
seeking a shade of Truth no one ever offered,
quite. Nowadays world's end is a little further,
and the chapel a housing estate.

Twins

They are caught unexpectedly,
eyes wide to camera,
inclined to giggle, but wary.
In those days, twins were an oddity,
butt of too many well-meaning jokes.
One wears her father's postman cap.
Though I am daughter and niece
even I cannot tell which is which.
In my childhood they were identical
still, but different, positive and negative.
It was not always so.
Before the winds of experience
flipped their lives about,
negative and positive made one whole.
So which is which here?
If only one of them had added a caption,
identifying self from other self. As it is,
I do not know my inheritance.

Woman and Man

She runs towards him,
clutching her jacket tight,
while the daisies she has picked
scatter in a chain of delight.
Even in black and white her face is flushed.
Her head is turned from him, modesty
forbidding too obvious a pleasure.
Only a fool would love a soldier.
In days he will be gone,
to march across murdering fields,
but she cannot help her joy.
My mother's cousin – friend?
I have no idea.
Her story haunts me,
though I shall never know its end.

Airman in Front of a Pyramid

'Lew in Egypt, 1942'
For once I have a date, a name:
the brother they both adored,
the only one to go off to fight –
though in a pay tent behind the lines.
Thin, bank-clerk legs
bronzed in baggy uniform shorts,
he looks happy,
fitter than in any peacetime pose.
For him war meant opportunity,
to travel, to write,
to make his pilgrimage to holy places
heard of in chapel. This is no portrait of a hero,
just a snap of an ordinary man
learning to endure other people's politics,
and for an hour or so
having the time of his life.

Postcard of Singapore

Tall towers glowing,
eyes in the sky watching,
the city floats,
reflected in sea and air.
Green, yellow, cerise,
lights shimmer, drag fingers of colour
across ink filled water.
They probe sullen craft, cramped
in a sullen harbour.
Train tracks rattle towards suburbs
crowding beyond the towers,
always onward.
A stormy dawn troubles the sky,
presses like a lid on roof and tower.
As I turn the card over
my own handwriting surprises.
When I scribbled that greeting
I never dreamt it would be treasured so,
a book-mark to separate the years.

Young Man standing at a Studio Table

He was handsome then –
enough to part inseparables –
before the creeping sickness
twisted mouth and hand.
His eyes suggest intelligence,
his expression, laughter;
a confident young man
looking towards life and love.
So much waste,
so much promise unfulfilled,
unless you count courage,
and the kind of staying power
that insists on wearing collar and tie,
when even to fasten a button
takes ten minutes.

AMERICAN RELATIONS

Each Christmas, my Grandmother
would unglue a wodge of currants,
flat-packed to her through a war
and beyond. "The American Relations,"
my Mother would whisper,
as if links to G.I.s and Bogart films
made blood bluer than majesty.

Gran's sister had helped populate
a continent, creating an address book
of second cousins as she moved from state
to state. I would have liked to claim her,
but all I knew was a box brownie photo –
a neat lady with one of her daughters,
revisiting England and finding it damp.

When they left, Gran's walnut tea caddy
sailed with them, some recompense
for all that dried fruit. Half a lifetime
later it sat on a Florida piano
while the daughter entertained me.
Eyes hazed by skies brighter
than mine, she saw by memory:

snow and fire and poison berries,
even the Klu Klux Klan, "uppettity
men" to her. Her words drew her mother
too, the indomitable Mary,
cooking on deck above an ocean.
Much divided us – segregation,
Viet Nam, – but being Family,

we fumbled across the gaps between.
Soon afterwards, her letters stopped,
and the next generation was busy.
Today fruit fills our supermarkets,
and guests find American relations
an uneasy theme. I sometimes wonder
– What happened to the tea caddy?

BEYOND CAPE CANAVERAL

We saw no rocket launches,
Astronauts, nor ticker-tape parades,
just an Armadillo – chain mailed,
pottering, an over-fed rat

with pigs' ears and dog's claws
– a pinch-nosed, long-tailed,
Friday afternoon bodge;
one of Nature's jokes.

Sensing aliens,
it shuttered into a ball,
bone-hard, impenetrable,
like an upturned basin

dropped in the gutter.
Amused, we waited,
until at last, unrolling,
it considered us

and we considered it.
Then, perhaps deciding
we were no more than
giant weeds, it scuffled on.

Odd how I can scarce recall
the lie of road or shopping mall,
but still see that Armadillo,
dust-baked, snuffling in a gutter.

FROM THE FRONTIER

Greetings, sister.
The socks you sent last month have been much worn.
Winter is cruel here, colder than any plunge pool.
Blood stiffens like the trees. Ice leaves
hang white against a bloated, frozen sun.
Sandals cannot keep this land out,
nor even regimental cloaks.

Since I last wrote we have built
another mile of wall – stone on stone –
and fought our first barbarians, wild men but deadly,
rising through mist and rain without a sound,
then disappearing as suddenly. I am learning to hate,
– and to fear, though I admit that only to you.
My men must think me impervious, like the rock
we hack into shape. We drink beer for courage
and play dice much of the night.
Sometimes we talk of home, but not often.
A wound is best left to heal.

How goes the election?
Who does Father favour? We hear little but gossip here,
and the winds' moan. If the gods permit,
I will last this year out,
then take my pension and plot of land in Dacia.
My little pagan wife promises to go with me.
We will grow olives and vines and children –
if I do not die of cold before.

And how are you?
You write little of yourself,
though you must be quite grown by now.
Send me the socks soon, Sister, I beg you,
and use my name often to others,
lest I be totally forgotten.

ISOLA TIBERINA

Two days ago, the Tiber barely flowed.
Where emperors and popes disembarked,
a treacle of silt and sewage struggled.
Now we walk the same riverside path
and find a night's rain in distant hills
has made the Tiber great again.
A seething lion of a river, it tears at sludge,
paws at bridges. Awed, we stop,
and watch water surge.

Isola Tiberina – it looks ordinary
enough, home for a hospital,
the usual church, yet round this spot
an empire began. My mind is as tired
as my feet. Facts and names
clatter like pebbles. Even the art is
unfamiliar here: marble conquests,
arrogance on horseback, perfection
as cold as economics.

And all those painted saints –
a Puritan childhood closes many doors.
Some day I must push those doors ajar.
This is my past too. Even in my bleak
northern home some exiled centurion
built a villa. (One broken pillar lingers.)
For now though, it is enough
to laze against a sunny wall,
while History slides beneath.

CAPITOLINE

They stack Time here like wedding cake,
layer upon layer. Cable men
dig trenches through roofs two metres
down while tramps sleep, unwitting
beside Nero's Golden House.

The Capitoline was prime real estate,
a Whitehall, Washington,
Kremlin in one, designed to awe rebels
and subdue the masses. Its architects
assumed crowd control.

With a hundred and fifty thousand
unemployed, free corn and games
were self-defence. Even then,
a high wall must be built, to separate
the festering from Government Hill.

I should be photographing happily,
but find I do not like the view.
The light is wrong, the stones obstruct.
I am too far outside that barricade –
wrong sex, wrong class, wrong politics.

STATUETTE

The child is held in a circle of care:
Father, Saint, Madonna,
each blurs into the other, absorbed in
stone's balance and rough-hewn pedestal.
Light gleams on poised heads, carves
shoulders, arms, folds of dress.

Yet this perfect symmetry remains
unnamed. No ego here, no medieval Dali
demanding a place in whispering halls.
This timeless grace seeks no fame,
was sculptured for the joy of it,
and to fill a niche on a chapel wall.

REFLECTIONS

Today
the world has inverted.
Mountains float downwards,
trees reach up to pebbles,
plait reeds, frame setting sun.
A swan glides beneath its shadow,
clouds slide beyond my feet.

For one rare,
tranquil moment, nothing
disturbs a mirrored afternoon.
I am Alice, in Looking Glass Land.
If I move very slowly, my other self
and I may clasp fingers,
across a universe.

ON SHORE TERMINAL

Like a horned beetle
the terminal squats, brutal, impersonal.
Water laps, oil clad, staining a concrete shore.
Once, oystercatchers dabbled here.
There are no birds now.

All is sterile symmetry.
Carried by an evening wind, reflections slide
sideways, doubling a concrete tower
and massive pipes. Nothing else moves.
Here oil is King.

Fishermen sold their boats
years ago, and sought southern jobs.
The waders fled too. A rhythmic plod of pumps
plays nightsong now. Some day, perhaps, historians
will find walls and pipes

sunk in sand,
and speculate a temple and wrathful gods.
How else could they explain such annihilation
of all things natural – for a mere stream
rising beneath a darkening sea?

FLAMINGOS

They dabble and surge in their thousands,
living candyfloss against a haze of sky.
High-steppers, they walk on water,
mirage-breakers, hoovering salt.

Their plenty amazes:
a profusion of grace and gossip.
Necks pattern and unpattern,
spider legs flicker across sun and lake.

A month of drought to come
they must risk a long march into night,
a silent column seeking remembered water;
chicks and aged will straggle unto death.

Today, though, they recall a world
before Man, a dabbling plenitude
of DNA, natural selection in motion;
absurdity in pink, against a prehistoric sky.

HANNAH NOAH SPEAKS

Last year he swore the sun would tumble
and burn us all, then he dreamt the waves stopped
and fish froze solid. This spring, his fear was
a Great Flood. "The world will drown,"
he predicted, "every living thing."
I called him a fool and went to feed the goats.

Then I found him lugging trees down the cattle byre.
His eyes were hollows filled with light.
"I'm mekking a boat," he snarled –
the prow stretched right down our barn.
Nor could he rest until our sons had joined him.
Their hammers hurt my brain –
and the cows bellowing, wanting milking,
with only me aware.

I killed the goats on my own too, my hair
gobbed with blood. We must take one pair of all
our stock he said. The rest must be salted down.
So I hacked and chopped and boiled
and could not stop shivering.

The neighbours laughed as we passed,
until a plug fell out the clouds.
In an hour the drains were fountains.
By nightfall, water was crumbling our walls.
The lights died, but I could hear the terror next door
and how they scrambled for chairs and mats
anything that would float.

Noah was aflame then, shouting and praying
– useless. I had to grab the children and fill the water jars
and stack the food, and stop Shem's wife from screaming.
We forced a hundred hands away when we launched,
slithering down our lawn ...

My sister's face will always float before me.

Two weeks ago the rains stopped. Now
the great lake recedes. We creep between stumps of walls,
through mud and carcasses. Soon we must hit ground
and scramble to begin anew. It is easier to drift
with an acceptable routine. The silence hurts though;
a few bleatings, a cough or two, the creak of canvass ...
little else. Even Noah has stopped asking, "Why us?"
just sits against the hay, watching the rainbow.

Perhaps others live beyond the rim of sky,
but though we watch hour upon hour,
no vessel passes us, on this vast, filthy sea.

OYSTER WOMAN

Nowadays,
she keeps things
to herself.

Thoughts are dangerous.
They provoke her man.
So she wraps them round

the grit of her life;
dreams may become
pearl some day.

Until then,
she smiles.
An oyster learns

to cling, unnoticed,
knowing the tide
cannot tear her away.

VOICES OFF STAGE

1. Cook to the Capulets

They wanted the stars for her –
an only one, pretty as stained glass.
She had a poor man's livelihood spent on her:
singing masters, fine silks to wear, a tame bear
– her father even taught her how to read.
We thought her spoilt, but she charmed us into care.
The grooms adored her, and that fat old Nurse
stayed instead of seeking better-paid positions.

And what did the silly girl do? Fall in love –
with a Montague. Everyone below stairs knew it;
we gossiped over supper, feared trouble would come of it,
but that fool of a nurse must have her Romance,
dream the immovable could be moved. I warned her myself.
"The boy's a threat," I said, "To himself, as well as Juliet,
climbing the cedar to turn her head, playing stupid songs
where our Master can hear. He'll get a sword in his gut.

"For his sake as well as ours send him packing."
But Nurse wouldn't listen. "Love will find a way,"
she canted. "No, it won't," I predicted –
"not now, when hate corrodes like poison."
And poison everything it did, including our sweet
Juliet. The house mourns; silence shrouds our meals.
I cook little now, and each morning, Nurse runs
to the bedchamber, and finds her baby gone.

2. Drawing Master to Richard III

Tonight I will draw him: a determined,
sunbound boy, riding life full pelt,
scattering old men's fears behind him.
I shall add no wizened hump. Let those
who would deceive, paint untruth,

not me. I saw only a curve of spine
such as might come from too much study.
"He'll be no weakling," I promised,
and Richard proved me right, practising
his sword like a musician perfects his piece.

He could draw well enough
but it was the mad ride he loved best.
"Careful!" I shouted, but the boy laughed,
clearing a five-bar gate. If his brother had lived –
and a crown not hung for the picking –

History would have recalled a brave soldier,
no monster. It grieves me still to picture him,
desperate, his horse dying beneath him,
and knowing his name would be deformed
like his corpse.

Time, you have painted him tyrant –
I will draw the man I knew.

3. Lady Macbeth's Sister

When we were small, you elbowed me out
– you were always the greedy one.
You would cap the jester, dance faster,
higher. Father encouraged you,
wanted soft beds for us both,
a warm Hall, wine, security.

I would not flatter a hideous king
and dreaded the jewelled dagger,
the childbearing to raise only a name.
So I settled for a shrewd trader
who would grow rich without being hanged.
You, Sister, wanted Power, Fame.

So you set your traps for a brave Thane
and snared him with ease. Poor man,
he was besotted. You could embroider
a tale or a brocade, smile when it suited,
beguile the storm away. Soon neither
Cawdor nor Glamis was enough.

Macbeth might have stayed honest
on his own – true – but when a fool peers
into a chasm, any push may send him over,
and you wanted what he desired.
I can admit that now,
from the safety of thirty years.

You paid terribly for your love –
and I must believe that you loved him,
or else all was waste, terrible, awful
waste. Sister, I dream of you often.
We throw quoits, and you leap up,
like an arrowed deer.

URBAN FOXES

His shadow crosses
the street, a Pictish invader
colonising daylight.
Grown old and unwise,
he trots between council estate
and curry shop, bold as the rats
whose runs he follows.
A rust-red silhouette,
he scents Ma Harris' tea.

Sitting in his unlicensed taxi,
Ted, Ed, Fred (whatever name
he is today), watches him pass.
He has his own cunning –
knowing the rat runs between
supermarket and station –
respects cunning in others,
is wise to the lad
who vaporises past his window.

Ratfaced Nick, still barely fifteen,
sensing he is watched,
pulls his cap back over hair
as red as any fox, and melts
into privet hedge.
Five minutes later, an alarm wails,
ignored. By then, Ted and Nick
are no where, and the fox
crosses an empty street.

SCHOOL PHOTOS

The gymslip is a shapeless bag.
Trapped in darned stockings, hair scraped
behind me, I pose, ambitious to please.
Soon, the boys will pull my plaits
and I will kick in return. Already,
one bow slides undone.

Another day, another school. This year
we sit in rows, smiles freezing to camera.
Leaves congeal in perpetual summer;
beyond them, railings spike distance.
Iron gates clang offstage, recalling
a scared child playing afternoon truant.

Here – Grammar Bug and Swot –
eleven-plussed out of class and family,
I stand in my squeaky blazer like a green wasp –
a first day image snapped by a jealous father.
The hat pretends Girls' Own stories,
the satchel is too new, the plait still slides undone.

In this last, the blazer is acceptably faded,
worn cuffs further up arms. The eyes
are defiant, looking out of their skull box,
challenging a world to disagree. Three rows
of similar cocksure, yet unsure, achievers
surround me, destined to claim a suburban lawn.

Some of us did scrabble further though,
giving thanks for gifts grudgingly received.
We confessed it at the Reunion – once we knew
who was who. That was when I revisited –
rarely a good idea. The Infants had become
a motorway; the Junior upwardly mobile,

but the Grammar School comped on.
I wonder if they still sanctify speech days,
a hockey-faced Head Girl serving piety
and plates of bourbons.
And do they still sing the old school song
in Black-Country Latin?

PEACOCK ON A LIBRARY ROOF

Gaudy enquirer, do you laugh at us?
You, with your iridescent punk head,
your jade flame of a neck?

Do mere humans amuse
slotted in desks
beneath your preening gaze?

We must seek inspiration,
but you simply stretch, to spread
rainbows across a window.

You distract, and surely
know it, flickering
an eyelid flirtatiously —

a gigolo of the bird race,
strutting your stuff on a library roof.
I haven't a chance against you.

SHADOW SHAPES

Summer will end now.
The craneflies are patterning,
pattering my lamp all night.
They skitter the ceiling,
dart at hair and eyes.

Betrayed by light,
some fizz in sacrifice,
or fly a fool's game,
across and across my room.
Rainsmoke swirls outside;

the old harp of chimney
and window frame plays
requiem. Yet two craneflies
settle beside me.
Quivering in delight

they mate, shadow shapes
matched in fragile elegance.
Even as death is preparing,
desire holds them, insists on
another year, another generation.

CONTINUITY

"You doant want weeds like these,"
Uncle warned.
"They'll tek years to fruit."
Yanking at damson suckers
as if eighty summers were mere greenfly,
he threw each spindly tree aside.
But we, being young in hope and gardening,
saved two from fire and compost.
They travelled a climate, and rooted.

For ten years our damson trees
have struggled, bent and withered,
born a sleet of blossom but little else.
One year we had five whole damsons;
another, enough for a Sunday pie.
Then suddenly, this profusion.
My basket cuts my arm,
the ladder will not reach.
Windfalls hide among our broccoli.

Now both uncle and parent tree are gone,
one dead, the other
cut down by new owners, nice people
who turn orchards into strips of lawn.
Yet Uncle's weeds grow sturdily,
memorials in leaf and bough.
Stronger than the ash that fell to fungus,
than the poplar blown across our door,
they bear fruit a thousandfold.

THE GROTTOES OF CATULLUS: FOR MY MOTHER

'At the extremity of a long and low peninsula....'

The guide book is quaintly lyrical,
translated from the Italian.
It directs us to ruins, pink as the cliff beneath,
and on, to arched passage ways,
grottoes of stone. We stand amazed,
in vaults higher than most hotels.
Pigeons mate on roofless walls.
Cryptoporticus, Peristyle, Triclinium
– air-conditioned or heated according to season –
each is numbered on our diagram.
This was no villa, but a palace, visited
by Emporers, home of Catullus himself
– so legend says.

We are early.
Behind us, modern Sirmione
prepares the day's tourist boats.
Here, the grove is quiet.
Lizards flicker on ancient stones;
Rosemary scents the air.
Along boughs older than the Crusades,
olives swell slowly.
Did Catullus really stand here,
looking out over lake and mountain?
I try to recall poems of love
revered by a bully of a master
a Grammar School ago.

At once I am a girl again, in battered hat
and woolly stockings, crammed
with ambition and useless knowledge.
Plucking a sprig of summer-dry rosemary,
I prick myself on past disappointment.
The pain is keen, blotting out sun and rock.
It becomes not just mine, but yours too,
Mother, and all those before us.
Grandad walked for days to preach
a Second Coming that never came.
Uncle wrote stories in a war-time tent –
his talent dried behind an office door.

Last week I found your photograph.
Only the caption told me it was you:
'Edith – aged sixteen, Crichieth'.
I rarely saw that eager smile.
To me you were Edie, the Good Woman,
called to nurse ancient aunts,
and manage on 'next to nothing'.
But what else might you have been,
had not war and work withered hope?
You had needs too – though you were
not the sort to voice them, suspecting
emotion as much as alcohol.

Odd, that a box-brownie snap
should return to me here.
A pair of firecrests flit
between silver leaves,
their tiny heads flashing red.
Fifty metres below, motor boats
draw lines across a page of lake,
while three white swans float
above a shelf of rock, each stroke
of leg and neck vivid in green water.
Yet I am Latitudes away,
trying to learn a mother years dead.

In your bleak last days,
closed round by age and infirmity,
Endurance became your theme.
You did not go gently into any good night,
but aware of your dying, and hating it.
Still you did not complain,
and still the staff thought well of you.
I began to like you then.
Whatever my ending.
I hope I can show your courage,
or at least your determination.
I shall not live up to your expectations
– or those you have bequeathed to me –

but here beside ruins and olive trees,
they matter less. It is sufficient to watch
the beauty of swans in green water,
while firecrests flash among silver leaves.

SIRMIONE

The Easter crowds pass, and pass
again, through gap-toothed gates.
They pause for coffee, or pray
at the shrine of Saint Anne.
An ooze of laughter and chatter
flows through every narrow street,
past china shops and cafés,
towards the lake.

Today is Sunday best.
High heels and city shoes
clack on cobbled steps.
Glimpses of water and boats
tantalise beyond flowered yards;
the ice parlour and church above
are breathless, airtight
with custom.

A stolid yellow castle broods,
still linking lake and land.
Beneath its bridge, tripper boats
queue and swans glide, where once
captives counted the oar's stroke,
or stared at sheer wall and iron grill.
Scaligeri – even the name
sounds ominous.

They ruled peasant and Pope,
built war machines of stone,
stamped their dues on goods
and traveller. But Time plays jester,
wags a pig's bladder at Power
and Pride. Now crowds
surge through their fortresses,
sucking ice cream.

WAR CEMETERY

We pay our ten pence, take a card
and walk through silence, past
a marble corpse, dead centre in a deadly space.
The sun touches rows of graves,
glints on silver birch, yellows yellowing leaves.

My mind cannot translate sums
that question arithmetic. How many?
Almost five thousand ... dying on English soil,
and buried here on Cannock Chase.
Erich Faust UFFZ,

Konrad Rudowski, OBLT...
Four to the slab they lie, two names to the front,
two at the back, in letters carefully measured,
spaced, chiselled. Anton, Georg,
Gerardus, Hermann ...

Names and rank bewilder, dazzle
in English sun. A few frail posies
splash colour against regimental stones.
Who came here to place their roses,
these dying chrysanths?

Anton, Georg, Gerardus, Hermann ...
And just as neatly, laid out in German fields,
Anthony, George, Gerald, Harry lie.
Separated by a narrow sea,
their graves glint in September sun.

CANDLES

I have carried many candles down my life,
lighting fiestas through darkened streets.
Across my childhood,
a stone sink reflects a jam-jarred end,
Birthday tables glow, stairs flicker.
Pumpkin faces warm my Halloweens,
and each Christingle reminds of other aisles
where light stains stone and frosted glass,
and friends greet me from arch and pew.

But tonight, as I light this frail taper,
my coin clangs into emptiness.
I would honour you, the ones
who happened to be there
when the final code rang. I dare not
imagine your last confusion –
the panic on the stairs, the stuck elevator.
Though light stains stone and frosted glass,
shadows mock from arch and pew.

JUST ANOTHER NEWS ITEM

Trimly built, bearded,
a pale studious face –
the defendant scribbles a note,
looks up, cleans his glasses.

Our minds slide sideways,
will not focus. That desiccated voice
belongs to academia, not a murder trial.
Such an ordinary little man

and yet so many deaths,
so many lives ended between two
and four, on sunny afternoons –
ladies in comfortable arm chairs ...

No doubt they thanked him,
apologised for being a nuisance.
How do those of us who remain cope,
explain the inexplicable?

THE NIGHT CAFÉ: VINCENT VAN GOGH, 1888

Drinkers slump in corners, harsh lights
dazzle above a monstrous table;
a man in white watches.
Bilious yellow – the nausea of night
caught in swirling strokes ...

The image is familiar.
Reduced to postcard respectability,
it lurks on gallery shelves, coffee tables,
examination rooms, yet still it shocks.
Biographies give time and circumstance

but do not prepare for such casual,
commonplace despair. The floor escapes
its frame, sliding towards us. A clock
is fixed forever at twelve fifteen a.m.
Most of us have passed a night here,

though in other cities, other times.
Even in faded print, Vincent's nightmare
touches ours. Stare, and dimensions blur,
until we, too, plunge towards that gaping,
curtained, room beyond.

LUPINS

Lupins flamed in the gardens
of her childhood; red, blue, orange,
slender torches lighting faded walls.
Each summer they flared
between notices sanctifying grass.
A few sturdy delinquents
strayed along railway lines,
rampaged demolition sites.

Uncle George grew lupins too,
elegant spikes groomed daily –
each floweret a tiny blue-tongued lizard
sunning itself in a judge's praise.
Lupins nodded near the french windows
the day he chased her round the settee
and caught her – just in fun –
his Sunday joke ... their secret.

Now, twenty years on,
she cannot see those niggling,
thrusting, tongues without shuddering.
Last night she found a whole border
lurking in a council park, gaudy as sin.
She trampled and trampled,
high heels piercing soil and flower
and stalk. Not one survived.

TOWTON

"There was a great conflict, which began with the rising of the sun, and lasted until the tenth hour of the night ..."
George Neville, Chancellor of England, reporting the battle of Towton in 1461.

Can you not see us? –
You – in the comfort of your car?
Look beyond your misted window,
beyond the wind-scarred cross
and you will find Palmsunday Field.
There, where rain knifes barren soil.

Can you not hear us? We were the luckless,
the liverymen, Yorkists left without shelter,
Lancastrians too poor for armour,
pressed to fight our masters' quarrel,
that left thirty thousand dead,
here, on a single, bitter, day.

Surely you recall *us*? – Lords in splendour,
cousin fighting cousin, and learning only
how snow churned to red, how men
slithered as they ran. They trampled a bridge
of their own dead to cross Cock Beck,
there – beyond Bloody Meadow.

Our bones trouble this land: the noble
as well as the lowly: sons avenging fathers,
to be avenged themselves three battles after.
You hurtle past and see only dash-board clock
and rise of road. We beseech you, pause
a moment. Remember us.